THE
AUTUMN EQUINOX
Celebrating the Harvest

Ellen Jackson

Illustrated by Jan Davey Ellis

THE MILLBROOK PRESS
BROOKFIELD, CONNECTICUT

TO SUSANNE HAMMEL-SAWYER
—E. J.

FOR MARK
—J. D. E.

Library of Congress Cataloging-in-Publication Data
Jackson, Ellen B., 1943–
The autumn equinox : celebrating the harvest / by Ellen Jackson;
illustrated by Jan Davey Ellis.
p. cm.
Includes bibliographical references.
Summary: Discusses the significance of some of the harvest festivals
around the world and describes how they are celebrated.
ISBN 0-7613-1354-0 (lib. bdg.) 0-7613-1442-3 (trade)
1. Harvest festivals—Juvenile literature. [1. Harvest festivals.
2. Festivals. 3. Holidays.] I. Ellis, Jan Davey, ill. II. Title.
GT4380.J33   2000 394.264—dc21
00-020169

Published by The Millbrook Press, Inc.
2 Old New Milford Road
Brookfield, Connecticut 06804
www.millbrookpress.com

THE AUTUMN EQUINOX

In most places on Earth, weather changes as the seasons change. These changes are caused by the tilt of the Earth's axis relative to the sun. In the summer when the Northern Hemisphere of the Earth is tilted toward the sun, the northern part of the world receives more sunlight. Daylight lingers into the evening hours and the weather is mild and warm.

In winter, the opposite is true. The Northern Hemisphere is tilted away from the sun and receives less sunlight. The sun sets much earlier, and winter nights are long, cold, and dark.

But on one day during the third week of September, daylight hours and nighttime hours are about equal. We call that day the autumn equinox. The word equinox comes from a Latin word that means "time of equal days and nights." This is the first day of autumn in the Northern Hemisphere.

In autumn, daylight decreases day by day, the weather grows colder, and the growing season winds down. Just as spring is the time for planting, autumn is the time of harvest. Today, as in the past, a series of harvest festivals brightens this season of increasing darkness.

Thanksgiving! Family and friends have come together. A white tablecloth covers the old oak table. The centerpiece, a horn of plenty, overflows with apples, grapes, nuts, and corn. Delicious aromas drift from the kitchen—roast turkey, potatoes, and pumpkin pie. Dinner is almost ready.

Thanksgiving is a harvest festival. When the tang of autumn is in the air, people in the United States and, on a different date, people in Canada gather to give thanks for the fruits and vegetables, the nuts and grains, and the many treasures of the fertile earth.

Harvest festivals date back to a time when people first began to grow their own food. To ancient people, a successful harvest was a matter of life or death. If crops were damaged by early frost or rain, entire families might go hungry or starve. Everyone worried about the winter ahead:

Onion skins, very thin,
mild winter coming in;
Onion skins thick and tough,
coming winter cold and rough.
        —*Old English Proverb*

At the time of the autumn equinox, the entire community helped bring in the harvest. People worked during the day, and they continued working at night when the bright harvest moon shone down upon the fields.

Children worked alongside their parents, helping their mothers bind the grain into bundles. After the crop had been harvested, the children gathered the stray ears of corn or stalks of wheat that had been left behind. When the work was done, everyone celebrated.

A successful harvest was a happy occasion. Ancient people held festivals to honor the spirits or gods who brought forth food from the earth. The Greeks gave thanks to Demeter, goddess of agriculture and grain. The Romans worshiped Ceres, the goddess of the corn. Her festival was held each year in October and included music, games and sports, and a thanksgiving feast. Our word "cereal" comes from the name of this goddess.

Long ago, the Chinese relied on the movement and phases of the moon to tell them when planting and harvesting should begin. The Chinese called the moon the Queen of Heaven, and they celebrated her birthday soon after the autumn equinox. To prepare for this holiday, special birthday cakes, round as the moon, were baked from the newly harvested rice. At midnight, when the moon was at its brightest, families gathered to eat the cakes and honor the Queen of Heaven and the Hare of the Moon, her rabbit companion.

The Chinese also believed that flowers fell from the moon on this night. It was said that men who saw the blossoms would be rich, and women who saw them would be blessed with many children.

The Celts, a people who lived in Great Britain and France more than two thousand years ago, observed only two seasons of the year—summer and winter. Samhain, a Celtic festival that occurred at the end of October, marked the end of the summer season and the beginning of winter. But Samhain was not part of either season and was considered outside of time. It was both a harvest festival and an occasion to honor the dead.

The Celts thought that on Samhain the spirits of the dead fled the barren fields and came back to visit their living relatives. Places were set at the table for members of the family who had recently died, and food was left for wandering spirits.

On Samhain, the Celts lit bonfires on the tops of hills to honor the gods. The villagers took embers from the bonfires back home, carrying them in scooped-out turnips or gourds. To frighten evil spirits that might be wandering around, the villagers dressed in costumes and carved scary faces on their gourds. Some of these customs eventually gave rise to modern Halloween traditions.

The Germanic people of northern Europe also believed that hostile spirits walked the earth at harvest time. They thought that invisible creatures or animals—gigantic pigs, rabbits, or foxes—might be hiding among the waving grain. After the harvest, the last sheaf of grain was dressed in clothes and placed on a wagon where people laughed and made fun of it. They believed that the spirits of the field had finally been defeated.

Even after the harvest was completed, people trembled when the autumn winds blew. They were afraid that Odin, the father of the gods, wanted part of the bounty. From the roofs of their houses people emptied sacks of flour into the wind so that Odin could have his share.

In England, farmers provided a feast of goose, roast beef, and plum pudding for the harvesters who had helped in the fields. In some places, the last load of corn was decorated with flags and flowers and taken around the parish while the harvesters shouted and sang. Then they drenched the corn with water to show that they no longer needed to worry that the crop would be damaged by early rain or frost. This was their way of saying, "Let the rains come now. We don't care."

The village church was decorated with autumn flowers, red apples, golden grain, and orange pumpkins. A loaf of bread, baked from the freshly harvested wheat, was placed on the altar, and people thanked God for the harvest.

The feast shared by the Pilgrims and Indians in the autumn of 1621 was actually a harvest festival similar to those held in England. The Pilgrims were particularly happy that they had survived their first year in a new land. They were also grateful for the advice and help of the Wampanoag Indians, who had shown them which wild berries were safe to eat and had taught them how to grow corn, squash, and beans in the new land.

The Pilgrims decided to hold a feast and invite their Indian friends. About fifty Pilgrims and ninety Indians took part in the celebration, which continued for three days. Wild turkey, ducks, geese, and deer meat, or venison, were served.

The Pilgrims' celebration was not the first harvest festival held in America. Hundreds of years before the arrival of the Europeans, Native Americans held harvest celebrations and special celebrations of thanksgiving throughout the year.

The Iroquois, a Native American people who lived in the eastern United States and Canada, performed a Green Corn Dance to give thanks for the ripening of the corn. The dancers were accompanied by singers who also played the water drum and rattles. Corn soup and bread were served, and children played lacrosse, a ball game still enjoyed today. The games and feasting continued for four days.

Like the Iroquois, the Yoruba of Nigeria, West Africa, held special dances in October at the time of the yam harvest. The dancers wore long robes and masks to represent the spirits of the ancestors. They danced in the street and visited the families of those who had died during the year. Newly harvested yams were offered to the dancers before the families were allowed to eat them.

The Jews also remember their ancestors at harvest time. Sukkot is an ancient Jewish harvest festival still celebrated today. During this festival, Jews everywhere thank God for the harvest and for their homeland of Israel. Little huts made from the branches of trees are set up in courtyards, in gardens, or on porches. The huts are decorated with fruits, berries, and wreaths of flowers and covered loosely with evergreen branches. They remind the Jewish people of the time when their ancestors wandered in the desert after the Exodus from Egypt and built makeshift huts out of palm leaves and branches.

Pongal is a three-day harvest festival of southern India. The festival, held in January, honors the sun and rain that ripen the rice crops. To prepare for Pongal, people paint designs on the walls and floors of their houses. Families cook newly harvested rice in milk. As soon as the rice begins to bubble, they cry, "Pongal!" which means, "It boils!" Then they add honey, raisins, and butter to make a tasty treat. On the third day of Pongal, Indians honor the cattle. They decorate their horns with fruit and flowers.

While many harvest festivals are celebrations for the entire family, children in Angola have a harvest festival of their own. Each child gathers ripe corn from the field. Then all the children meet in the woods near a stream. They light fires and roast corn on the cob. Everyone tries to steal corn from everyone else. It's all part of the fun!

Today in North America and parts of Europe, bringing in the harvest is no longer a community project. Now machines do almost all the work. Huge combines cut the wheat and separate it from its hard outer covering. Using special attachments, these machines also harvest corn, soybeans, and rice. Food can be shipped around the world in a matter of days using new methods of packaging and transportation. Supermarkets offer bananas from South America, tea from India, and oranges from California.

In spite of these changes, people everywhere still celebrate the harvest. It's a time to be grateful for the many wonderful foods that come to us from all over the world. It's a time to remember how much we depend on the earth and its many gifts.

AN AUTUMN STORY

*The Calumet, or peace pipe, was a sacred object to the
Sac and Fox Nation, called the Sauk, a North American people
originally living in Michigan, Wisconsin, and Illinois. The
following story was adapted from a Sauk legend.*

When the Great Spirit had made the earth and all living
beings, he seated himself by a lake and admired his cre-
ation. He saw that the water of the river ran cold and clear,
and wild flowers bloomed in the meadows.

But something was missing. The Great Spirit filled his
pipe and took a long smoke. Soon hazy wisps floated over
the woods, the prairies, and the lakes.

A ribbon of smoke circled the hickories, aspens, and
poplars and turned their leaves to gold. The smoke brushed
the oak, and its leaves changed to pinkish brown. Sumacs,

flowering dogwoods, and gums blazed red, and green maple leaves deepened to scarlet.

The smoke passed over the rugged mountains and through the dark forests. Vines grew thick with grapes, and tree branches put forth nuts and fruits for the animals and birds.

Then the leaves let go of their hold and floated to earth one-by-one. Men and women filled great baskets with yellow ears of corn, grain, and squash. A huge orange moon peered over the edge of the world.

Thus the fire of life flared up with all the colors of autumn, and the Great Spirit provided a final feast for his children. Then with icy breath, the Great Spirit covered the earth with a blanket of frost.

The harvest was over. Winter had come.

CLASSROOM ACTIVITIES*

A HARVEST OF CHILDREN

You will need:

a large map of the world
thumbtacks with colored heads
yarn
3- x 5-inch (7.5- x 13-cm) cards

1. Have the children ask their parents and relatives to list the homelands of their ancestors.
2. Display a large map of the world on a bulletin board.
3. Locate the school on the map, and mark it with a thumbtack with a colored head.
4. Each child should locate his or her ancestral country on the map. Mark the country with the child's name or with another colored tack. A piece of yarn should connect the tack marking the country with the tack marking the school.
5. After each child has selected a country of origin, have him or her research a few interesting facts about that country. Write the facts on cards and place the cards around the map. Share the research with the class.

CHINESE MOON CAKES

You will need:

prepackaged or homemade cookie dough
jam
sesame seeds
round cookie cutters
rolling pins, cookie sheets, knives, etc.

1. Roll out the dough with the rolling pin.
2. Cut out the dough with the cookie cutters.
3. Bake at 375 degrees for 8 to 12 minutes. Cool.
4. Spread with jam and sprinkle with sesame seeds.

* Although these activities are planned for teachers, many of them can be easily adapted as hands-on projects for the individual child at home.

THANKERCHIEF

You will need:
a handkerchief

Children sit in a circle. A handkerchief is passed around the circle, and the children chant: "Pilgrims, pumpkins, one-two-three. Here is what they mean to me." The child who has the "thankerchief" when the chant ends tells one thing that he or she is thankful for.

SWEET APPLES WITH CINNAMON

The following is a wonderful harvest snack that will serve sixteen children. Double the recipe for a class of thirty-two.

You will need:

8 apples
1 cup (240 milliliters) raisins or currants
2 teaspoons (10 milliliters) lemon juice
1 cup brown sugar
2 tablespoons (30 milliliters) melted butter
cinnamon
vanilla ice cream
melon scoop
baking pan

1. Cut apples in half and use the melon scoop to hollow out a portion of each half. Mix raisins, lemon juice, brown sugar, and melted butter.

2. Fill each apple half with the mixture.

3. Place each half in a baking pan and sprinkle with cinnamon.

4. Bake at 350 degrees for 30 minutes until tender.

5. Serve warm with vanilla ice cream

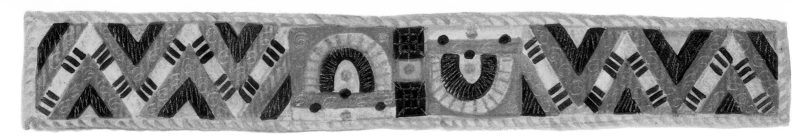

AFRICAN HARVEST DRUM

For each drum you will need:

1 16-ounce (454-gram) tin can
2 9-inch (23-cm) round
    balloons
masking tape

tissue paper
starch
yarn
wooden chopsticks (optional)

1. Remove the top and bottom from the tin can.
2. Cut the necks off two round balloons. The bulb of each balloon should be large enough to stretch over one end of the can, capping it and lying flat. Secure each balloon by taping it in place with masking tape.
3. Hold a twig or wooden chopstick in one hand and twist the severed neck of one of the balloons over the end to make the head of the drum stick.
4. Dip strips of tissue paper in starch. Cover the body of the can with the strips of paper.
5. Dip pieces of yarn in starch and decorate the body of the can with African symbols.

A NOTE OF THANKS

You will need:

slips of paper
pencils
ready-to-bake crescent rolls

1. Each child writes something that he or she is thankful for on a slip of paper.
2. The teacher gathers the slips of paper and rolls each up into an unbaked crescent roll.
3. Bake rolls. When the children open the rolls, they read the enclosed slips of paper to the class.
4. Everyone eats the rolls.

SUKKAH
(Shelter for the Jewish Sukkot Festival)

You will need:

tissue boxes or shoe boxes
scissors
colored tissue paper
paste
starch

magazines
paper punch
straws
twigs and leaves

1. To make the Sukkah, use tissue boxes with the tops cut off or shoe boxes without the lids.

2. Cut a square opening in the side for the door.

3. Cover the sides of the box with tissue paper dipped in starch. You can also use construction paper. Decorate the inside of the boxes with pictures of flowers, fruits, and vegetables cut from magazines.

4. Punch parallel holes with a paper punch at regular intervals across the two long sides of each box. The holes should be about ½ inch (1 cm) from the top. Push straws through the holes. Lay a loose covering of leaves and twigs on top.

A PONGAL DESSERT

This recipe serves eight to ten

You will need:

1 cup (240 milliliters) cooked rice
1 cup of milk
½ cup (120 milliliters) unsalted chopped
    almonds or cashews
½ cup raisins or currants
1 teaspoon (5 milliliters) honey
saucepan

1.   Cook milk in a saucepan. Stir frequently until mixture comes to a boil.
2.   Say, "Pongal!"
3.   Add rice, chopped nuts, raisins, and honey
4.   Stir and cook on low heat 5 to 10 minutes longer until the milk has been absorbed.
5.   Enjoy.

NATIVE KNOW-HOW

A Native American named Squanto showed the Pilgrims how to grow corn by using fish as fertilizer. The following activity demonstrates this method.

You will need:

two Styrofoam cups
potting soil
corn seeds
pens
fish fertilizer
graph paper
water

1.   Fill two Styrofoam cups almost to the top with potting soil. Plant a corn seed in each.
2.   Draw a fish on the side of one of the cups.
3.   Water the fish cup with water that contains fish fertilizer for household plants (available at any gardening store). Follow the directions on the bottle before watering.
4.   Water the other cup with plain water.
5.   In a few days, the seeds will sprout.
6.   Have the children graph the growth of the two plants.

BIBLIOGRAPHY

Budd, Lillian. *Full Moons: Indian Legends of the Seasons.* New York: Rand McNally & Company, 1971.

Epstein, Sam and Beryl. *European Folk Festivals.* Champaign, IL: Garrard Publishing Company, 1968.

Helfman, Elizabeth S. *Celebrating Nature: Rites and Ceremonies Around the World.* New York: The Seabury Press, 1969.

Henes, Donna. *Occasions: Seasons, Cycles and Celebrations.* New York: The Berkeley Publishing Company, 1996.

James, Edwin Oliver. *Seasonal Feasts and Festivals.* New York: Barnes and Noble, Inc., 1962.

Kalman, Bobbie, and Susan Hughes. *We Celebrate the Harvest.* New York: Crabtree Publishing Company, 1986.

Markle, Sandra. *Exploring Autumn.* New York: Atheneum, 1991.

Pegg, Bob. *Rites and Riots: Folk Customs of Britain and Europe.* Poole, Dorset, England: Blandford Press, 1981.

Rosen, Mike. *Autumn Festivals.* New York: The Bookwright Press, 1990.

Whitlock, Ralph. *Thanksgiving and Harvest.* Vero Beach, FL: Rourke Enterprises, Inc., 1987.

ABOUT THE AUTHOR AND ILLUSTRATOR

Author Ellen Jackson has written more than forty fiction and nonfiction books for children. Her best-selling *Cinder Edna* has won many awards, as has *Brown Cow, Green Grass, Yellow Mellow Sun*. A former elementary school teacher who now writes full-time, she lives in Santa Barbara, California, where she enjoys exploring tide pools along the shore.

Columbus, Ohio artist Jan Davey Ellis has illustrated many successful books, among the most recent being *The Quilt Block History of Pioneer Days with Projects Kids Can Make* and *A Sampler View of Colonial Life with Projects Kids Can Make*, both by Mary Cobb, and *Hasty Pudding, Johnnycakes, and Other Good Stuff: Cooking in Colonial America* by Loretta Ichord.

The author and artist together have created *The Winter Solstice*, which was a Children's Choice selection of the International Reading Association/Children's Book Council. They are now at work on *The Summer Solstice* as well as *The Spring Equinox*. Their most recent collaboration, *Turn of the Century*, received a starred review from Booklist and a pointered review from Kirkus.